CONTENTS

LAKE CLASSICS

*Great American
Short Stories I*

WITHDRAWN

Bret

HARTE

Stories retold by Janice Greene
Illustrated by James Balkovek

LAKE EDUCATION
Belmont, California

LAKE CLASSICS

Great American Short Stories I

Washington Irving, Nathaniel Hawthorne, Mark Twain, Bret Harte, Edgar Allan Poe, Kate Chopin, Willa Cather, Sarah Orne Jewett, Sherwood Anderson, Charles W. Chesnutt

Great American Short Stories II

Herman Melville, Stephen Crane, Ambrose Bierce, Jack London, Edith Wharton, Charlotte Perkins Gilman, Frank R. Stockton, Hamlin Garland, O. Henry, Richard Harding Davis

Great British and Irish Short Stories

Arthur Conan Doyle, Saki (H. H. Munro), Rudyard Kipling, Katherine Mansfield, Thomas Hardy, E. M. Forster, Robert Louis Stevenson, H. G. Wells, John Galsworthy, James Joyce

Great Short Stories from Around the World

Guy de Maupassant, Anton Chekhov, Leo Tolstoy, Selma Lagerlöf, Alphonse Daudet, Mori Ogwai, Leopoldo Alas, Rabindranath Tagore, Fyodor Dostoevsky, Honoré de Balzac

Cover and Text Designer: Diann Abbott

Library of Congress Catalog Number: 94-075015
ISBN 1-56103-005-8
Printed in the United States of America
1 9 8 7 6 5 4 3 2 1

🌿 Lake Classic Short Stories 🌿

"The universe is made of stories, not atoms."
—Muriel Rukeyser

"The story's about you."
—Horace

Everyone loves a good story. It is hard to think of a friendlier introduction to classic literature. For one thing, short stories are *short*—quick to get into and easy to finish. Of all the literary forms, the short story is the least intimidating and the most approachable.

Great literature is an important part of our human heritage. In the belief that this heritage belongs to everyone, *Lake Classic Short Stories* are adapted for today's readers. Lengthy sentences and paragraphs are shortened. Archaic words are replaced. Modern punctuation and spellings are used. Many of the longer stories are abridged. In all the stories, painstaking care has been taken to preserve the author's unique voice.

Lake Classic Short Stories have something for everyone. The hundreds of stories in the collection cover a broad terrain of themes, story types, and styles. Literary merit was a deciding factor in story selection. But no story was included unless it was as enjoyable as it was instructive. And special priority was given to stories that shine light on the human condition.

Each book in the *Lake Classic Short Stories* is devoted to the work of a single author. Little-known stories of merit are included with famous old favorites. Taken as a whole, the collected authors and stories make up a rich and diverse sampler of the story-teller's art.

Lake Classic Short Stories guarantee a great reading experience. Readers who look for common interests, concerns, and experiences are sure to find them. Readers who bring their own gifts of perception and appreciation to the stories will be doubly rewarded.

❦ Bret Harte ❧
(1836–1902)

About the Author

Many of Bret Harte's best stories are set in the bars, country stores, and gold mining towns of the Old West. Local color was his specialty. Harte was born in Albany, New York, some 25 years before the Civil War. He moved to California when he was 18.

In San Francisco, Harte made himself the leader of a brilliant group of young writers. Along with Mark Twain, Ambrose Bierce, and others, he helped to make San Francisco the literary capital of the West.

Today, Harte is best remembered for two short stories he wrote in 1868 and 1869. These stories, *The Luck of Roaring Camp* and *The Outcasts of Poker Flat,* brought him national fame. Readers loved his colorful characters and vivid descriptions of life in the mining camps.

In 1871, Harte moved to New York on a high tide of popularity. There, the temptations of fame proved too much for him: His work dropped off and his debts piled up. He had never been a well-balanced personality. Mark Twain called him "one of the pleasantest men I have ever known; also one of the unpleasantest." In 1877 he moved to Europe, where he remained for the last 24 years of his life. Although little known, some of the stories Harte wrote in his later life were better-written than his earlier stories. *An Ingenue of the Sierras* is one of these.

Harte's work is still recognized for its technical skill. By starting the local color school in American fiction, he set new standards for the short-story art form.

If you want to see the Old West through the eyes of a man who saw it in person, you'll enjoy reading Bret Harte.

The Outcasts of Poker Flat

Do you think there's such a thing as a good person with a bad reputation? This is a famous story of generosity and courage in the Old West. The action takes place on a journey across the Sierra Mountains. The unlikely hero is a gambler who has to make a life-or-death decision when the chips are down.

THE LEADER OF THE ARMED MEN GAVE A FINAL WARNING.
IF THE OUTCASTS CAME BACK, THEY WOULD BE KILLED.

The Outcasts of Poker Flat

Mr. John Oakhurst, gambler, stepped into the main street of Poker Flat. It was the morning of November 23, 1850. He could tell at once that something was different. Something about the town had changed since last night. Two or three men were talking together. When they saw Mr. Oakhurst coming, they suddenly stopped and looked at each other. There was a Sabbath quiet in the air, which was very strange for Poker Flat. Things did not look good for Mr. Oakhurst.

But Mr. Oakhurst's handsome face did not look worried. "I reckon they're after somebody," he thought, "probably me." He stopped to clean the red dirt of Poker Flat off his boots. Then he put his handkerchief back in his pocket and went on his way.

In fact, Poker Flat *was* "after somebody." Not long ago, the town had lost several thousand dollars, two good horses, and a very important person. Now, a secret group had been formed. The members of this group wanted to get rid of all the "no-good" people in Poker Flat. Already, two men had been hanged. Now they were going to drive the rest of the unwanted people out of town.

Mr. Oakhurst was right. Poker Flat wanted to get rid of him, too. Some people in the secret group thought he should be hanged. They wanted to get back the money he had won from them. One of the group, Jim Wheeler, said, "It's not right! We can't let this young man—a stranger from Roaring Camp—carry away our money!" But a few men had been lucky enough to win money from Mr. Oakhurst. They said it wouldn't be quite fair to hang him.

Mr. Oakhurst listened to all this talk with a cool and quiet mind. He was a gambler, after all. He knew he had to play the cards he'd been given. And he knew the dealer would always have a little over him.

A group of armed men led the outcasts out of Poker Flat. Besides Mr. Oakhurst, there were two women who had worked in the bar. One was a young woman called "the Duchess." The other woman was called "Mother Shipton." And there was "Uncle Billy." People thought he *might* have robbed gold from the miners. And they knew for sure he was a drunk.

As the outcasts were led by, the people of Poker Flat watched without a word. At the edge of town, the leader of the armed men gave a final warning. His words were few, and to the point: If the outcasts came back, they would be killed.

Then the armed men rode off, leaving the outcasts alone. The Duchess cried wildly. She said she would die on the road. Mother Shipton went on and on about cutting someone's heart out. Uncle Billy swore. Only Mr. Oakhurst said nothing. With the easy good will of a gambler, he turned to the Duchess. He traded his own horse, Five Spot, for her sorry mule.

The outcasts made their way down the road toward Sandy Bar. That town lay on the other side of the mountains. Getting there was a hard, day-long trip on a thin trail.

Soon they passed out of the warm hills and up into the mountains. The air turned cold and dry. Finally, at noon, the Duchess rolled off her horse and onto the ground. She would not go another step, she said.

The spot where they stopped was wild and beautiful. It was a flat place, with many pine trees. On three sides there were high stone cliffs. The last side was a long, downward slope to a valley. It was a good spot for a camp—if camping had been a good idea. But it was not. They were not even halfway to Sandy Bar. Mr. Oakhurst said it would be crazy to stop. He pointed out that they had no food, nothing to cook with, no warm clothes. "Why throw in your hand before the game is played out?" he said.

It was true that they did not have food, or warm things, or a plan. But they did have whiskey. Soon they didn't worry about anything else.

Mr. Oakhurst did not drink. As a gambler, he needed a clear head. When offered a drink, he always said he "couldn't afford it." He sat away from the rest. For the first time, the life he had led felt like a heavy load. He made himself get up and clean the dust from his black clothes. He washed his face and hands. That made him feel a little better. He looked around at the high walls of rock above him and the cloudy sky above the rock. Suddenly, he heard his name called.

A man was slowly riding up the trail. It was Tom Simpson of Sandy Bar. He was called "the Innocent." Some months ago, Mr. Oakhurst had met the Innocent over a "little game." He had taken $40 from the young man. It was all the money the Innocent had. When the game was finished, Mr. Oakhurst took the other card player behind the door. He said, "Tommy, you're a good little man. But you can't gamble worth a cent. Don't try it again." Then he gave Tom Simpson all his money back. After that, the young man would do anything for Mr. Oakhurst.

The Innocent said *hello* in a voice that sounded like a boy. He said he was on his way to Poker Flat—to live there.

"Alone?" asked Mr. Oakhurst.

"No, not exactly alone," said the Innocent with a giggle. He said he had come with a girl called Piney Woods. Did Mr. Oakhurst remember her? She used to wait on tables at the Temperance House. Old Jake Woods, Piney's father, hadn't wanted him to marry her. So Tom and Piney had run away—and here they were. They were tired out, but they felt lucky to have found a camp, and people to be with.

Then Piney rode up. She had been hiding behind a tree, her face pink and happy-looking. She was a big, good-looking girl of 15.

Mr. Oakhurst wasn't happy about mixing Tom and Piney with the likes of him and the other outcasts. As Piney came up, Uncle Billy was about to say something rude. Mr. Oakhurst gave him a kick to keep him quiet.

At first Mr. Oakhurst tried to talk the Innocent into going straight on to Poker Flat. He pointed out that he and the others had no food, and no way to make a camp.

But the Innocent said he had an extra mule, which was loaded with food. He was happy to share everything. Also, he and Piney had found a log hut near the trail. "Piney can sleep in there with Mrs. Oakhurst," said the Innocent. He pointed to the Duchess. Uncle Billy was about to burst into a roar of laughter.

Mr. Oakhurst gave him another kick. So
Uncle Billy walked off and told his joke
to the tall pine trees, slapping his leg.
When he came back, everyone was
sitting together. They had made a fire,
for the air now had a strange chill in it.
Piney was talking to the Duchess. The
Innocent was talking to Mr. Oakhurst
and Mother Shipton. Everyone seemed
to be having a good time.

"Is this here a picnic?" mumbled Uncle
Billy. He looked at the group and the
dancing fire. Then he looked behind
them, at the tied-up animals. Suddenly
an idea came to him. The idea must
have been a funny one, for he slapped
his leg again.

The shadows moved slowly up the side
of the mountain. A light wind rocked the
pine trees and made them moan. It grew
dark. Mr. Oakhurst and the Innocent
covered the holes in the log hut with pine
branches. It was ready for the ladies.
Piney and the Innocent said goodnight
with a kiss. The kiss was so honest and
sweet it might have been heard above the

pine trees. The Duchess and Mother Shipton stared at the pair without a word. They were probably too surprised to say anything. The men lay down in front of the door. In a few minutes they were asleep.

Mr. Oakhurst was a light sleeper. Before morning he woke up, feeling cold. He poked at the fire. Then he felt something on his cheek—something that made his cheek turn white. It was snow!

He jumped up. He knew they had to hurry now. There was no time to lose. Then he saw the place where Uncle Billy had been sleeping. The old man was gone. He ran to the spot where the mules had been tied. But they, too, had disappeared.

Mr. Oakhurst walked quietly back to the fire. Careful not to wake the others, he pulled his blanket around him and waited for the morning. Dawn came slowly, with blowing snow. The land all around them was changed. Mr. Oakhurst took all this in and said just two words, "Snowed in!"

The food had been inside the log house—safe from Uncle Billy's sticky fingers. Mr. Oakhurst figured that if they were careful, they had enough food to last ten more days.

But for some strange reason, Mr. Oakhurst could not make himself tell the Innocent what Uncle Billy had done. Instead, he said that Uncle Billy had walked off from camp and scared the mules by accident. He told the Duchess and Mother Shipton not to tell, either. "If they find out anything, they'll find out the truth about *all* of us. It's no good making them scared now," he said.

The Innocent was not worried. "We'll have a good camp for a week," he said. "Then the snow will melt, and we'll all go back together."

The young man was so happy, it made the others happy, too. He put up more pine branches to make a roof for the hut. The Duchess fixed up the inside of the hut in a very nice way. What she did made Piney's blue eyes open wide. "I reckon you're used to fine things in Poker Flat," the girl said. The Duchess turned away quickly. She didn't want Piney to see that her face was red. Mother Shipton asked Piney not to "chatter."

When Mr. Oakhurst came back from looking for the trail, he heard the sound of happy laughter. His first thought was of the whiskey. He thought he had put it where no one could find it. "But somehow it doesn't sound like drink," he said to himself. Then he looked through the falling snow at the fire and the people around it. It seemed like they were just having "square fun."

Maybe Mr. Oakhurst hid his cards along with the drink. Maybe not. But he didn't say the word *"cards"* all that long night.

The time was passed with the help of an accordion that the Innocent had in his pack. Piney Woods played several songs with it. The Innocent played along with a pair of bone castanets. But the best part of the evening came when they sang a camp-meeting hymn. The Innocent and Piney joined hands and sang loudly. At last the others joined in to sing along:

"I'm proud to live in the service of the Lord,

And I'm bound to die in His army."

Above them, the pines rocked and the storm blew hard.

By midnight, the storm stopped. The stars were bright above the sleeping camp. Mr. Oakhurst and the Innocent took turns standing watch. But, in the end, Mr. Oakhurst did most of it himself. He told the Innocent that he had "often been a week without sleep."

"Doing what?" asked the Innocent.

"Poker!" said Oakhurst. "When a man gets a streak of luck—real luck—he don't get tired. He waits for the luck to give in first.

"Luck is a mighty strange thing," he went on. "All you know for sure is that it's going to change. Finding out *when* it's going to change is what makes you. We've had a run of bad luck since we left

Poker Flat. You come along, and you get into it, too. If you can hold your cards right, you'll make it," said Oakhurst. Then, for no reason at all, he began to sing:

"I'm proud to live in the service of the Lord,
And I'm bound to die in His army."

The third day came. The sun rose as the outcasts were sharing their food for the morning meal. All around them the snow was high—a sea of white. They could look down on Poker Flat miles away. Mother Shipton saw the town and swore. Somehow shouting curses made her feel better. She told the Duchess, so that no one else could hear, "You just go out there and look at it. Then *swear.*"

That night they tried the accordion again. But now the music was not enough. They were hungry. Then Piney thought of something new—telling stories. Mr. Oakhurst and the women had no wish to tell any stories of their own. But a few months ago, the Innocent had read the *Iliad*. So now he told the story, in the style of Sandy Bar. For the rest of the night, the heroes of the *Iliad* walked the earth. Mr. Oakhurst liked the story. He especially wanted to know what would happen to "Ash-heels," which was the Innocent's name for "Achilles."

In that way—with little food and much of the *Iliad* and some of the accordion— a week went by. Another storm came. Day by day, the walls of snow grew higher around them. It became harder and harder to get wood for the fire. But Piney and the Innocent still turned away from the snowy wall, looked into each other's eyes, and were happy. Mr. Oakhurst set himself coolly to the losing game before him. The Duchess took care of Piney. Only Mother Shipton, who had been the strongest, grew sick and weak.

At midnight on the tenth day, she called Oakhurst to her side. "I'm going," she said. "But don't say anything about it. Don't wake the kids. Take the bundle from under my head and open it."

Mr. Oakhurst did so. Inside was Mother Shipton's food for the week. She had not even touched it.

"Give it to the child," she said. She pointed to Piney.

"You've starved yourself," said the gambler.

"That's what they call it," said the woman in a sharp voice. Then she turned her face to the wall and quietly passed away.

The accordion and the bones were put aside that day. The *Iliad* was forgotten. Mother's Shipton's body was buried deep in the snow. Then Mr. Oakhurst had a quiet talk with the Innocent. He showed him a pair of snowshoes he made from an old pack-saddle.

"There's one chance in a hundred to save Piney," he said. "But you've got that chance, if you can make it to Poker Flat. If you can get there in two days, she's safe."

"And you?" asked the Innocent.

"I'll stay here," he said.

Piney and the Innocent held each other for a long time.

The Duchess saw Oakhurst getting ready to leave. "You're not going, too?" she asked.

"Just for a little way," said Oakhurst. Then he turned suddenly and kissed her. Her white face turned to fire. Her arms and legs shook with surprise.

Night came, but not Mr. Oakhurst. It brought the storm again, and wild, flying snow. The Duchess kept the fire going. She found that someone had put enough wood for a few more days next to the house. Tears rose in her eyes, but she hid them from Piney.

The women did not sleep much. In the morning, they looked into each other's faces. They knew what was to come—but they said nothing. Piney, the stronger one, put her arm around the other woman's waist. They lay like this the rest of the day. That night the storm was even stronger and wilder than ever. It tore away the pine branches around the hut and blew snow inside.

Near morning, they could no longer feed the fire. Slowly, it died away. The Duchess spoke for the first time in many hours. She said: "Piney, can you pray?"

"No, dear," said Piney.

The Duchess did not know why, but this made her feel better. She put her head on Piney's shoulder and said nothing more.

They fell asleep. The wind grew quiet, as if it were afraid to wake them. Light snow blew down from the pine trees like white birds. It fell around the sleeping women.

They slept all that day and the next. They did not wake up when voices broke the quiet of the camp. Fingers gently brushed the snow from their faces. They both looked so peaceful, you could not tell which of the women had been the "bad" one. Even the lawmen of Poker Flat saw this. They turned away, and left the two in each other's arms.

But a little way from camp they found something else. On one of the largest pine trees they found a playing card—

the two of clubs. It was stuck to the tree with a bowie knife. Written in pencil on the card was this:

Beneath this tree
Lies the body
of
JOHN OAKHURST
Who struck a streak of bad luck
on the 23rd of November, 1850
and
Handed in his checks
on the 7th of December, 1850

Mr. Oakhurst lay there, cold, with a pistol by his side and a bullet in his heart. He was as calm in death as he was in life. In the end, John Oakhurst was both the strongest and the weakest of the outcasts of Poker Flat.

An Ingenue of the Sierras

Gangs of bandits often robbed stagecoaches in the Old West. Will Yuba Bill be able to outwit them? In this humorous tale, a pretty young woman holds the fate of all the passengers in her own small hands.

WE HEARD THAT THE RAMON MARTINEZ GANG MIGHT BE WAITING FOR US. WE KNEW THEY WOULD TRY TO TIME THE PASSAGE OF OUR LIGHTS ACROSS THE RIDGE.

An Ingenue of the Sierras

The stagecoach flew through the dark across Galloper's Ridge. We all held our breath. Anybody who was looking would have seen only a shadow. The coach's side-lights had been put out. One passenger had been smoking a cigar, to show how calm he was. But Yuba Bill had politely taken it from the man's lips.

We had heard that the Ramon Martinez gang might be waiting for us. We knew they would try to time the passage of our lights across the ridge. Then they would know just when to head us off into the brush. But if we could cross the ridge before they saw us, we'd be safe.

The huge coach rolled along through the dark. Yuba Bill kept it safely on the track. As the Expressman said, Bill could "feel and smell" the road he could no longer see. We knew that at times we hung over the edge of the ridge. We also knew that it was a drop of at least a thousand feet to the trees below. But Bill knew that, too. The horses cut through the dark like a plow.

Finally the ridge was crossed. We drove into the even darker brush. Somehow it seemed that we were no longer moving, but instead, the night was flying by us. One of the passengers said in a whisper, "Suppose we meet another team—going as fast as we are!" To our great surprise, Bill heard it. We were even more surprised when he spoke. "If we did meet another team," he said quietly, "it would be a neck and neck race. We'd see who could reach the devil first!" But we all felt better—for the silent man had said *something*.

Suddenly, we could see the wide road up ahead. We were out of danger.

So we lit the lamps again and everyone started talking. We told Yuba Bill what a fine job he'd done. But he said nothing. For some reason he seemed sad, even angry.

"I guess the old man was ready for a fight," one passenger said. "Now he's sorry there isn't one." But some of us knew Bill. He had the true spirit of a fighter. He'd never want to fight without a good reason.

The Expressman said, "You ain't worried about anything, are you, Bill?"

Bill lifted his eyes. "Not about anything *to come*. It's what *has* happened that don't make sense to me. I don't see no signs of Ramon's gang ever having been out at all. And if they were out, I don't see why they didn't go for us."

"It seems simple enough to me," one of the passengers said. "Our plan worked.

They waited to see our lights on the ridge. When they didn't see them, they missed us until we had passed. That's my opinion."

"You ain't putting any price on that opinion, are you?" asked Bill politely.

"No," said the passenger.

"Good," Bill said. "Because there's a comic paper in 'Frisco that pays for opinions like that."

We all laughed.

"Come off it, Bill," said the passenger. "Then why did you put out the lights?"

"Well, it might have been because of you passengers," Bill said. "I didn't want you shooting away at some bush you *thought* was moving. That would have brought down their fire on us."

We weren't sure if we should believe that or not. We thought we'd better accept it with a laugh.

Then Bill turned to the Expressman. "Who got in at the Summit?" he asked.

"Derrick and Simpson of Cold Spring, and one of the 'Excelsior' boys," the Expressman answered.

"And that Pike County girl from Dow's Flat, with her luggage," a passenger added. "Don't forget *her*."

"Does anybody here know her?" Bill said.

"You'd better ask Judge Thompson," a passenger said. "He was awful helpful to her. He got her a seat by the window and looked after her luggage and things."

"Got her a seat by the *window*?" repeated Bill.

"Yes," said the passenger. "She said that she wanted to see everything. Said she wasn't afraid of any shooting."

"Right," said another passenger. "And was he ever helpful to her! When she dropped her ring, he lit a match to look for it. That was against your rules. And that happened just while we were crossing through the brush, too. I saw the whole thing. I was hanging over the wheels, with my gun ready for action. We were lucky the Judge didn't show us up, and get us a shot from the gang."

Bill said nothing. He drove on.

Now we were about a mile from the station, where we would change horses.

We were driving through a stand of pine trees. Then all at once a man on a horse rode up. He seemed to be a "packer," or mule-driver.

"Hello!" said Bill. "You didn't get held up back there?"

"No," said the packer, with a laugh. "I don't carry anything a gang would want to steal. But I see you got through safe, too. I saw you crossing over Galloper's Ridge."

"*Saw* us?" Bill said in a sharp voice. "We had our lights out."

"Yes, but I saw something white—a handkerchief or woman's veil, I reckon. It was hanging from the window. It was only a moving spot in the dark. But I was looking out for you, and I knew you by that. Good night!"

He rode away. We wondered what Bill was thinking. He didn't say a word until we reached the station. Then he stopped and threw down the horses' reins. The passengers climbed out of the coach and walked toward the station. When the

Expressman started to follow them, Bill stopped him.

"Before we leave here," Bill whispered, "I want to take a good look over this here coach—and these passengers, too."

"Why, Bill, what's up?" asked the Expressman.

Bill pulled off one of his big gloves. "Well," he said. "I saw something when we came down from Galloper's Ridge and passed into the brush. I saw a man—just as sure as I see you—rise up from the brush. I thought our time had come and the band was going to play. But the man sort of drew back. And just as we passed him, he made a sign."

"Well?" said the Expressman.

"Well," said Bill. "It means this here coach was *passed through free* tonight."

"You don't mind *that,* do you?" the Expressman said. "I thought we were pretty lucky."

Bill slowly pulled off his other glove. "I've been risking my life on this line three times a week," he said. "And I'm always glad for a little luck. But when it comes to being passed free by some pal of a horse thief, *I ain't in it!* No, sir, I *ain't in it!*"

* * * *

The passengers were told there would be an extra 15-minute wait at the station. Bill explained that the screw bolts had to be tightened. Some passengers weren't happy about the delay. They were in a hurry to get to Sugar Pine, where they could have breakfast. But others were happy to wait for daylight. They knew the road would be safer then.

The Expressman knew the delay had nothing to do with loose screw bolts. He knew Bill was angry about what had happened. But he didn't understand what good it would do to wait around.

The station was small. All that was there was a stable, a wagon shed, and a building. Inside the building was a large room where passengers could wait. Most of the passengers were in that room, sitting around the fire. Bill went in and joined them. He started to talk to Judge Thompson.

Before long the Judge admitted that he had helped the young woman. Yes, he had lit a match so she could find her ring. But the ring had only dropped in her lap. "What a fine, fit, young woman she is," the Judge went on. "She's a true prairie blossom! Yet as simple as a child! She said that she's on her way to Marysville. Then she's going to meet a friend later on."

At that Bill went out to join the young woman, who was out in the stable yard. He saw that she was a good-looking country girl, with honest gray eyes and a laughing mouth. Just as he walked up, workers were loading the bags on to the roof of the coach. One of her own trunks was being tossed up a bit roughly. She jumped a little as she saw it.

"Careful there!" Bill called to the worker. "You ain't lifting rocks! Look out, will you!"

Bill pushed the worker aside and picked up a large trunk. But his foot slipped. When the corner of the trunk hit the ground, the top snapped open. The trunk itself was a cheap thing. But inside it Bill could see a number of very fine lady's things. They were white and lacy. "Oh!" cried the young woman. She stepped forward.

Bill told her how sorry he was, as he tied the broken trunk with a strap. The coach company would "make it good" to her, he promised. He'd be sure that she'd get a new one.

He walked her to the waiting room. Then he went over to the youngest passenger, who was sitting in front of the fire. He lifted the young man up by his coat collar, so the pretty woman could take his seat.

The young woman watched Bill take his waybill from his pocket. "Your name is down here as Miss Mullins?" he asked.

"Yes," she answered. Then she noticed that all the passengers were looking at her. The color rose in her face.

"Well, Miss Mullins," Bill said, "I have a question or two to ask you. I'll ask it straight out in front of all these people. You don't have to answer if you don't want to. You've got a friend over there—Judge Thompson. He's a friend to you, right or wrong. So is every other man here. It's like you've packed your own jury. Well, the question I've got to ask you is *this*: "When we were on Galloper's Ridge, did you signal to anybody?"

We couldn't believe what we had heard. How could Bill ask a young lady such a thing in front of everyone? Especially this particular young lady—so young and good-looking and innocent?

"Really, Bill . . ." began the Judge.

"*I did,*" said the young woman.

"Ahem!" said the Judge. "That is—er—you let your handkerchief hang out the window. I saw it myself. I'm sure you didn't mean anything by it."

"I signaled," said the young woman in a firm voice.

"Who did you signal to?" Bill asked gravely.

"The young gentleman I'm going to marry," said the woman.

Some of the younger passengers giggled. Bill shut them up with an angry look.

"Why did you signal him?" Bill asked.

"To tell him I was here," the young woman said, "and that everything was all right." Her look was proud. The color was high in her face.

"That *what* was all right?" Bill demanded.

"That I wasn't followed," she went on. "And that he could meet me on the road beyond Cass's Ridge Station." She stopped a moment. Then with great pride in her young voice, she said, "I've run away from home to marry him. And I mean to do it! No one can stop me. Dad didn't like him just because he was poor—and Dad's got money. Dad wanted me to marry a man I hate. He got a lot of dresses and things to bribe me."

"And you're taking those things in your trunk to the other young man?" Bill asked.

"Yes," said the young woman. "I told you he's poor."

"Then your father's name is Mullins?" said Bill.

"It's not Mullins," she said. "I—I made up that name."

"What *is* your father's name?" Bill demanded.

"My father is Eli Hemmings," she said.

We all looked at each other with a smile. Eli, or "Skinner" Hemmings was well known as a miser and a loan shark. People far and wide knew about him.

Then Judge Thompson spoke. His voice sounded like a stern father, but it was also kind. "The step you are taking, Miss Mullins, is a very serious one," he said. "I hope you and your young man have thought about it. I don't want to get in the way. But what do you know of this—er—young gentleman? Have you known him long?"

"Oh, yes," she said. "Almost a whole year." The Judge smiled. "And is he in business?"

"Oh, yes. He's a collector."

"A collector?" said the Judge.

"Yes. He collects bills. You know—money," she went on, sounding like a child. "He doesn't collect for himself. *He* never has any money, poor Charley. He collects for his firm. It's awful hard work, too. It keeps him out for days and nights, over bad roads in the worst weather. Sometimes he used to sneak over to the ranch, just to see me. He'd be so worn out he'd almost be falling out of his saddle.

"The work he does is dangerous, too. Sometimes people get mad at him and won't pay. Once they shot him in the arm. That time he came to me at the ranch. I helped do it up for him. But he don't mind. He's real brave. Just as brave as he is good."

How true and honest she sounded. Our hearts went out to her.

The Judge asked gently, "What firm does he collect for?"

"I don't know exactly," she said. "He won't tell me. But I think it's a Spanish company. You see, I only know because once he got a letter from his boss. And I peeked at it. I think the name was Martinez. Yes, Ramon Martinez."

There was a dead quiet. Then one of the passengers burst into a loud laugh. But the angry eye of Yuba Bill made him suddenly quiet.

The young woman didn't seem to notice. "Yes, it's awful hard work he does," she went on. "But he says it's all for me. As soon as we're married, he's going to quit. Of course he could have quit before. But he won't take any of my money. That ain't his way.

"He's awful proud, my Charley. Why, there's all that money that Ma left me in the Savings Bank. I wanted to draw it out—I had the right. I would have given it to him. But he wouldn't hear of it! Why, he wouldn't take one of them things in my luggage, if he knew. So he goes on riding and riding—here, there and everywhere. And all the time getting more tired out and sad, and thin, and white as a spirit. He's always worrying about his firm. When we'd be together he'd suddenly start up and say, 'I must be going now.' I knew he was worried. But he always tries to act happy around me.

"Just think of it," the young woman went on. "Why, he must have rode miles and miles to see me pass over Galloper's Ridge. Just to see if I was safe. And Lordy! I would have given him the signal if I had to die for it. There! That's why I'm running away from home. It's because I'm running to him. And I don't care who knows it! I only wish I'd done it before. And I would have—if—if—he'd only *asked me*!" Then she stopped. And all at once, the tears came.

All of us men were helpless. We looked out the window. We blew our noses. We said, "Imagine that!" and "I say," to each other.

Yuba Bill kicked the logs in the fireplace. Then he got us all out on the road. Miss Mullins was left alone. He told us not to say another word to Miss Mullins about her "young man."

Then he and the Judge walked back into the waiting room. Soon, out they came, bringing Miss Mullins. How happy we were that she was no longer crying! When she climbed into the coach, we drove off without further delay.

The Expressman turned to Yuba Bill. "She don't know who her young man is?" he asked.

"No," said Yuba Bill.

"Are *you* sure it's one of the gang?" the Expressman asked.

"Can't say for *sure,*" Bill replied. "They say there was a new man when the gang pulled that job at Keeley's. I hear there was some buckshot unloaded on that job. That might match up with what the girl said about the wound on his arm."

"So what are you going to do about him?" the Expressman asked.

"I'll see what this fellow looks like first," Bill said.

"But you ain't going to try to take him, are you?" the Expressman asked in a worried tone. "That would be playing it pretty low down on them both."

"Keep your hair on, Jimmy!" Yuba Bill laughed. "The Judge and me are just going to wrestle with the spirit of that young galoot. If he'll come out and say he's done wrong—and find the Lord— then all right. We'll marry him and the gal at the next station. The Judge will do it for nothing. We're going to have this thing done right—you bet!"

"But what if he doesn't trust you?" the Expressman went on.

"Miss Mullins will signal to him that it's all square," Bill said.

"Ah!" said the Expressman. He looked as if he believed things might turn out all right after all.

Bill, on the other hand, seemed very sure of himself. He even had something like a smile on his face.

The stagecoach drove on. It was bright day on the mountain tops around us. But as we rolled down into the valleys, it was still dark. Lights were still on in the cabins and ranch buildings we passed. It was hard to see by the time we reached a little stand of trees. There the Judge passed a note up to Yuba Bill.

At once, Bill began to slow down the horses. The coach stopped near a crossroad. Miss Mullins quickly stepped down from the coach. She waved good-bye to the Judge, and then she walked over to the crossroad. It was too dark to see her for long.

To our surprise, the coach waited. Five minutes went by. It seemed like a long time to sit and wonder what was going on. But something in Yuba Bill's face kept us quiet.

At last, we heard a strange voice call from the road: "Go on—we'll ride behind you," the voice said.

Then the coach started forward. We heard the sound of wheels behind us. We turned around but it was too dark to see much. All we could make out was a buggy with two people in it. It must have been Miss Mullins and her young man! We hoped he would pass, but he did not.

Then the Expressman asked Bill, "Is this her young gentleman, then?"

"I reckon it is," said Bill.

"But what's to keep them from running off together now?" the Expressman wanted to know.

Bill jerked his hand toward the boot. "Their luggage," he said.

"Oh!" said the Expressman.

"Yes," said Bill. "We'll hang onto that gal's things until the marriage is done—just as if we was her own father. And what's more, you'll express them trunks through to Sacramento. She can get them *there*. That will keep him on the right path, and out of the reach of that gang."

Yuba Bill winked at the Expressman. "I'll tell you," he said, "I can fill the bill every time! When I sets up two young people who are starting out in life together, there's nothing cheap about my style."

The passengers could now see the settlement of Sugar Pine up ahead. The little buggy shot by us. It passed so quickly we could not see the face of the driver. Keeping far ahead, the couple drove up to the hotel and went inside.

Our coach stopped just as the breakfast bell rang. Everyone wanted a look at Miss Mullins' young man. But everyone was hungry, too. So as soon as the coach stopped, we all went quickly into the dining room. Bill and the Judge disappeared.

Our trip with Yuba Bill was over. Sugar Pine was as far as he drove. The coach that would take us to Marysville and Sacramento stood waiting as we ate breakfast.

Soon Yuba Bill and the Judge came out of the hotel. We rushed to the windows to get a look at Miss Mullins' new husband. He was a good-looking young man, even fine-looking. But his eyes were shifty. It was not a nice look to see in a man who had just been married.

But Miss Mullins looked so happy, so innocent, so full of joy, that our hearts went out to her once more.

We watched the couple get into their buggy and drive away. Then Yuba Bill led us to a sitting-room. The Judge was waiting there when we walked in.

"Gentlemen," Bill said, "you was all here at the start of this little game this morning. The Judge thinks you ought to be in on the end of it. So I've called you in here to take a drink to the health of Mr. and Mrs. Charley Byng. What you know or what you think about this young galoot isn't worth a thing. But the Judge thinks you ought to keep it in the dark. That's his opinion. As far as my opinion goes—" Bill smiled, "I just want to say, if I catch any one of you blathering idiots saying one word—"

"One moment, Bill," said the Judge with a serious smile. "I just want to say that no one here is going against the law. We have *no proof* that Mr. Byng has ever done anything wrong. All we have is the word of Miss Mullins. And her lips are shut forever—since she and Mr. Byng are now man and wife. So I think you should all be happy to keep quiet about this. And now let us drink to a happy life for both of those young people."

We were very glad to do as he asked. Then most of the passengers left to take the coach for Sacramento. We could see that Miss Mullins' luggage was already on the coach. Then the driver cracked the whip and the coach rolled away.

Standing in the empty bar with the Expressman, Yuba Bill was a happy man. He told the Expressman what had really happened with Miss Mullins and Mr. Charley Byng.

"You see," said Yuba Bill, "when old Bill takes hold of a job like this, he does it all the way—no changing horses. But for a while, I wasn't sure it would work. We thought we better make that young man tell his gal who he really was! If she'd hung back just a little, that would have been it. We would have given Mr. Byng five minutes to get up and leave her. And we would have taken that gal and her luggage back to her dad again!

"But when she saw him, she started laughing and crying both at once! She said that nothing would part the two of them again. Gosh! If I didn't think he was more cut up about it than she! For a minute it looked like *he* didn't want to marry her. But that passed. They was married hard and fast—you bet! I guess he's had enough of staying out nights. We've seen the last of one more of the Ramon Martinez gang."

"What's that about the Ramon Martinez gang?" asked a quiet voice.

Bill turned quickly. It was the voice of the Divisional Superintendent of the Express Company. This was one man Bill did not look down on.

The Superintendent came over to the bar. "You haven't seen one of the Ramon Martinez gang, have you?" he asked.

"No," said Bill. He held his glass up to the light.

"And believe me, you *won't,*" said the Superintendent with a wink. "The gang is just about finished. It's too hard for them to get money for the things they steal. They can't get rid of gold. When they bring it into an office, they have to show where it came from. They can't afford a good fence to bring it in. That would cost too much. It comes down to this: They can't melt it down themselves and they can't get others to do it for them. They can't take it to the Mint or Assay Offices in Marysville or 'Frisco. No one there will take it without our certificate or seals.

"No, sir," the Superintendent went on, "that gang is just about played out. And the proof is that they've been taking passengers' trunks lately. Just the other day there was a wagon held up near Dow's Flat. I had to go down there to look into it. They had stolen some luggage from that rich couple who got married at Marysville. Seems they ran off with a lot of woman's wedding things. Looks like they're getting pretty low down, don't it?"

The Expressman was looking at Bill. Bill was looking out the window. Then he slowly pulled on one of his big gloves and said in a slow voice, "You don't happen to know old 'Skinner' Hemmings over there, do you?"

"Yes," said the Superintendent.

"And his daughter?" said Bill.

"He hasn't got any daughter," said the Superintendent.

Bill's face seemed to go yellow. Then his voice came, slow as the devil. "A happy, innocent sort of child?" he asked.

"No, I tell you he doesn't *have* a daughter," the Superintendent said. "Old man Hemmings never got married. He's too cheap."

"And you didn't happen to know any of that gang, did you?" Bill said slowly.

"I knew every last one of them," the Superintendent said. "There was Frenchy Pete, Cherokee Bob, Kanaka Joe, One-eyed Stillson, Softy Brown, Spanish Jack, and two or three others."

"And you didn't know a man by the name of Charley Byng?" Bill said in a soft voice.

"No," said the Superintendent. He looked toward the door, as if he was ready to leave.

"Are you sure?" Bill asked. "A dark, good-looking man, with shifty eyes and a mustache that curls up?"

"No," said the Superintendent. "Look here, I'm in a little bit of a hurry. But I guess you must have your little joke before I leave. Now just what *is* your little game?"

"What do you mean?" said Bill in surprise.

The Superintendent said, "What do I mean? Well, old man, you know as well as I do. The only man in the gang who looks like that is Ramon Martinez himself! Ha! Ha! No, Bill! You didn't play me this time. You're clever, all right. But you didn't catch me this time."

The Superintendent moved away with a light laugh. Bill turned to the Expressman. His face was like stone. But then his sad eyes grew light with laughter. He whispered to the Expressman, "But I got even after all!"

"How?" said the Expressman.

"Now Martinez is tied up to that lying little she-devil, hard and fast!" Bill laughed.

How Santa Claus Came to Simpson's Bar

Life was often harsh in remote western towns—especially in the dead of winter. In the town of Simpson's Bar, most people's luck had been running bad. It seemed that Christmas would come and go like any other day. But that was before a sick little boy asked his father about Santa Claus.

"MA SAYS THAT EVERYWHERE ELSE BUT HERE PEOPLE
GET PRESENTS ON CHRISTMAS."

How Santa Claus Came to Simpson's Bar

It had been raining for a long time. Mud covered the mountain road that led to the little village called Simpson's Bar. The town was cut off from the world completely. No one could get to it, and no one could leave. It was Christmas Eve, 1862.

As night fell, most of the men of the town were gathered at Thompson's store. "The Old Man" came in. Like a chameleon, he could take on the shade and color of other people's moods and feelings. Laughing, he clapped the shoulder of the nearest man and threw himself into an empty chair.

"I just heard the funniest thing, boys! Jim Smiley was just telling the best story about—"

"Smiley's a fool," said one gloomy voice.

"He's a skunk," added another.

A cold silence followed these statements. The Old Man looked quickly around the group. Then his face slowly changed. "You're right," he said. "Smiley is a sort of skunk—and something of a fool, too. Of course." He was silent as he thought about what a bad fellow Smiley really was.

"Terrible weather, isn't it?" he added. "And tomorrow's Christmas. Yes, and tonight's Christmas Eve. How would all of you like to come to my house for a little visit?"

"Well, I don't know," said Tom Flynn with some interest. "What about your wife, Old Man? What does she say about it?"

Before the Old Man could answer, Joe Dimmick suggested strongly that it was "the Old Man's house," not his wife's. That meant that he could invite anyone he wanted—whether she liked it or not.

"Of course. Certainly. That's it," agreed the Old Man. "It's my own house. Didn't I build it myself? Don't you be afraid of her, boys."

Then Dick Bullen spoke up. "Old Man, how's your son Johnny getting along? He wasn't feeling well last time I saw him. Maybe we'd be in the way if he's sick?"

But the Old Man said quickly that Johnny was better and that a little fun might liven him up. Then Dick stood up. "I'm ready," he said. "Lead the way, Old Man." Before long, the men arrived at the Old Man's cabin.

"Wait here a minute, while I go in and see that things are all right," the Old Man said. The others waited outside, leaning against the wall and listening.

For a few moments there was no sound but the wind in the trees. Then the men got worried, and they started whispering to one another. "I reckon she's hit him over the head!" "Maybe

she's got him down and is sitting on him!"
"She's probably boiling something to throw on us."

Just then the door opened slowly, and a small boy looked out. "Come in out of the rain," he called. "The Old Man's in the kitchen talking to Ma."

The men sat around a long table in the center of the room. Johnny put a few things on the table. "There's whiskey. And crackers and cheese. Just help yourselves. I have to go back to bed."

"Why, what's up, old fellow?" asked Dick.

"I'm sick."

"How sick?"

"I've got a fever, and I ache all over."

There was a long silence. The men looked at each other and then at the fire. They slipped into a gloomy mood. But then the Old Man's voice came shouting from the kitchen.

"Certainly! Of course they are. A gang of lazy drunken bums—and that Dick Bullen's the worst of all. Imagine! Coming here with sickness in the house and no food. That's what I said. 'Bullen,' said I, 'you're either drunk or a fool, to think of such a thing.' But they just had to come—*had* to! That's what you can expect of such lazy trash!"

The men sitting around the table started laughing. Whether their laughter was heard in the kitchen was not clear. But the back door was suddenly slammed hard. A moment later, the Old Man came in, smiling.

"The old woman thought she'd just run over to Mrs. McFadden's for a visit," he said. Then he sat down at the table.

Some time later, close to midnight, Johnny called out, "Oh, Dad!"

"His rheumatism must be acting up again," the Old Man explained. "He needs a rubbing. Wait here, and I'll be back." The door to Johnny's room didn't quite close, so the men heard the following conversation.

"Now, sonny, where does it hurt?"

"From here to here. Rub here, Dad."

There was a silence as the Old Man rubbed his son's leg. Then Johnny said, "Having a good time out there, Dad?"

"Yes, sonny."

"Tomorrow's Christmas, isn't it?"

"Yes, sonny. How does it feel now?"

"Better. What's Christmas, anyway? What's it all about?"

"Oh, it's a day."

This explanation seemed to be enough for Johnny, for there was silence again. But then Johnny went on, "Ma says that everywhere else but here people get presents on Christmas. She says there's a man they call Sandy Claws who comes down the chimney on Christmas Eve. She says he gives things to children— boys like me. That's what she tried to tell me, Dad. She just made that up, didn't she?"

In the great quiet that followed, the wind in the pine trees was the only sound the men could hear.

Then Johnny said, "That's enough, Dad. I feel much better now. Will you sit with me until I go to sleep?" After a little while, the Old Man returned to the main room. To his surprise, everyone was gone but Dick Bullen.

"Where is everyone?" the Old Man asked.

"They've gone to get my horse. They'll be back in a minute. There, that's them now."

There was a low tap at the door. Dick Bullen opened it quickly, said good night to his host, and went out. Waiting for him were his friends and his horse, Jovita. "It's already past 12. Can you make it? It's 50 miles, round trip," said Staples.

"I reckon I can," said Dick.

"At five, we'll be waiting at the shallow part of the river. Go along now! GO!"

By 1:00, Dick Bullen could see Rattlesnake Creek at the bottom of the hill. The creek was flooded. But Dick was hoping that Jovita would pick up a lot of speed going down the hill. He hoped she would be going so fast she wouldn't be able to stop. And sure enough, when they got to the creek, Jovita dashed into the middle of the swift current. After a few moments of kicking, wading, and swimming, they reached the other side.

By 2:30, Dick reached Tuttleville and took a tour of the sleeping town. He stopped at several closed shops, knocked on the windows, and woke up the owners. By 3:00, he was back in the saddle. By now he had a small bag strapped on his shoulders.

Dick and Jovita rode hard. Before long they were just 30 minutes away from Rattlesnake Creek. It was then that a man suddenly leaped from the bushes and grabbed at Jovita's bit. Another man—this one on a horse—appeared in the road. "Hands up!" cried this second man.

Jovita shook her head and threw off the man holding her bit. Then she ran toward the man in front of her. A curse and a gunshot rang out. The next moment Jovita was 100 yards away. But the good right arm of her rider had been shattered by a bullet. The wounded arm dropped helplessly at Dick's side.

Dick moved the reins to his other hand and continued his ride. When he got to Rattlesnake Creek, he saw that it was twice the size it had been before. For the first time that night, Dick's heart sank.

But then he thought of the sleeping boy. With a shout, he dashed into the yellow water. A cry rose from the other side as Dick's friends watched what happened. The head of the man and the horse struggling against the current were swept away!

* * *

The Old Man started and woke. Somebody was knocking at the door. He opened it, and then fell back with a cry.

"Dick?"

"Hush! Is he awake yet?"

"Johnny? No. But Dick—what happened to you?"

"Dry up, you old fool!" Dick hissed. Then he almost fell, but caught himself at the handle of the door. "There's something in my pack here for Johnny. Take it off. I can't."

The Old Man took the pack and laid it on the floor.

"Open it, quick!"

He did so with trembling fingers. The pack contained only a few poor toys. All of them were cheap, but bright with paint and tinsel. One toy was broken. Another was ruined by water. On the third was a spot of blood.

"It doesn't look like much," said Dick, sadly. "But it's the best we could do. Take them, Old Man. Tell him Sandy Claws has come."

And so it was that Santa Claus, with one arm hanging helplessly at his side, came to Simpson's Bar. The Christmas dawn came slowly after Dick Bullen rode away. The pale winter sun touched the hills with the rosy warmth of its love. And it looked so tenderly on Simpson's Bar that the whole mountain blushed to the skies.

Thinking About
the Stories

The Outcasts of Poker Flat

1. Are there friends or enemies in this story? Who are they? What forces do you think keep the friends together and the enemies apart?

2. The plot is the series of events that takes place in a story. Usually, story events are linked in some way. Can you name an event in this story that was the cause of a later event?

3. Good writing always has an effect on the reader. How did you feel when you finished reading this story? Were you surprised, horrified, amused, sad, touched, or inspired? What elements in the story made you feel that way?

An Ingenue of the Sierras

1. Compare and contrast at least two characters in this story. In what ways are they alike? In what ways are they different?

2. An author builds the plot around the conflict in a story. In this story, what forces or characters are struggling against each other? How is the conflict finally resolved?

3. All stories fit into one or more categories. Is this story serious or funny? Would you call it an adventure, a love story, or a mystery? Is it a character study? Or is it simply a picture the author has painted of a certain time and place? Explain your thinking.

How Santa Claus Came to Simpson's Bar

1. Is there a hero in this story? A villain? Who are they? What did these characters do or say to form your opinion?

2. Imagine that you have been asked to write a short review of this story. In one or two sentences, tell what the story is about and why someone would enjoy reading it.

3. What period of time is covered in this story—an hour, a week, several years? What role, if any, does time play in the story?

Thinking About
the Book

1. Choose your favorite illustration in this book. Use this picture as a springboard to write a new story. Give the characters different names. Begin your story with something they are saying or thinking.

2. Compare the stories in this book. Which was the most interesting? Why? In what ways were they alike? In what ways different?

3. Good writers usually write about what they know best. If you wrote a story, what kind of characters would you create? What would be the setting?